CUB REPORTER MEETS FAMOUS AMERICANS

WHAT'S YOUR STORY, HELEN KELLER?

Emma Carlson Berne
illustrations by Doug Jones

Lerner Publications ◆ Minneapolis

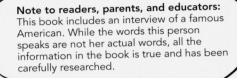

Note to readers, parents, and educators:
This book includes an interview of a famous American. While the words this person speaks are not her actual words, all the information in the book is true and has been carefully researched.

Lerner Publications Company
A division of Lerner Publishing Group, Inc.
241 First Avenue North
Minneapolis, MN 55401 USA

For reading levels and more information, look up this title at www.lernerbooks.com.

Main body text set in Avenir LT Pro 45 Book 15/21. Typeface provided by Linotype AG.

Library of Congress Cataloging-in-Publication Data

Berne, Emma Carlson.
　　What's your story, Helen Keller? / Emma Carlson Berne.
　　　　pages cm. — (Cub reporter meets famous Americans)
　　Audience: Grades K–3.
　　ISBN 978-1-4677-7968-5 (lb : alk. paper) — ISBN 978-1-4677-8539-6 (pb : alk. paper) — ISBN 978-1-4677-8540-2 (eb pdf)
　　　1. Keller, Helen, 1880–1968—Juvenile literature. 2. Deafblind women—United States—Biography—Juvenile literature. 3. Deafblind people—United States—Biography—Juvenile literature. 4. Sullivan, Annie, 1866–1936—Juvenile literature. I. Title.
　　HV1624.K4B442　2016
　　362.4'1092—dc23 [B]　　　　　　　　　　　　　　　　　2015000426

Manufactured in the United States of America
1 – VP – 7/15/15

Table of Contents

Helen Keller 4

Where and when were you born? 6

How did your illness change your life? 8

What was life like for other blind and deaf people
    in your time? 10

Who was Annie Sullivan? 12

What else did Annie teach you? 14

Did you go to school? 16

What was the Cambridge School like? 18

Where did you go to college? 20

What did you do after college? 22

How did you become famous?. 24

What were your biggest successes? 26

How did your work help other people? 28

Timeline 29

Glossary 30

Further Information 31

Index. 32

Hi, everyone! Today, I'm interviewing a very important person. Her name is Helen Keller. Helen, why are you famous? Can you tell us a little about yourself?

Helen says: I would love to! I was an **activist** for people with disabilities. I was also blind and deaf myself. Even though I couldn't see or hear, I learned how to read, write, and talk. This was difficult for a person with my **disabilities**.

As an adult, I worked to help other blind and deaf people. I gave speeches, wrote books, and traveled all around the world. I even appeared in movies!

Young Helen Keller sits
at her desk with a book.

Where and when were you born?

Helen says: I was born in 1880 on a small farm in Alabama. My family wasn't rich, but we did have a large house and a few servants to help us.

I was a smart and active little girl. But when I was a toddler, I became very sick. The illness hurt my eyes and my ears. When I got better, I couldn't see or hear anything.

Helen Keller *(left)* poses with her younger sister, Mildred.

Helen was raised in this house in Tuscumbia, Alabama.

How did your illness change your life?

Helen says: The illness left me permanently deaf and blind. My voice still worked. But I couldn't hear other people talking, so I couldn't learn to speak.

If I wanted something, I made hand motions that my family understood. But this worked only for very simple things, like when I wanted something to eat. I couldn't tell people what I was thinking. This made me very angry. I had terrible tantrums. Sometimes I would even break dishes and throw them across the room.

Helen, at aged seven, holds her pet dog.

What was life like for other blind and deaf people in your time?

Helen says: Today, deafblind people can go to school and have jobs. People with disabilities can live in their own homes, get married, and have children if they want to.

But when I was growing up, life was very difficult for people who were both blind and deaf. Not many schools taught deafblind people. Most deafblind people never learned to read, write, or speak. It was also hard for deafblind people to find jobs. Many people simply stayed home with their families. This is probably what my life would have been like—if I hadn't met an amazing person: my teacher, Annie Sullivan.

Perkins School for the Blind is in Watertown, Massachusetts. Helen sometimes took classes there.

Who was Annie Sullivan?

Helen says: Annie Sullivan was a very talented teacher. She was also mostly blind. When I was six years old, my parents asked her to be my teacher. She came to live with us. Annie helped me learn to communicate with other people.

Annie taught me words by tracing signs for letters on my hand. This was called the **manual** alphabet. I could spell words back to Annie by making signs into her hand. I learned hand spelling very quickly. Annie would tell others what I was saying. I could finally communicate with my family!

Helen *(left)* plays chess with her teacher, Annie Sullivan, in 1899.

What else did Annie teach you?

Helen says: She helped me learn to talk! She put my fingers on her mouth and throat. I felt her lips move when she said words. Then I tried to make those same movements with my own mouth. I could also feel **vibrations** in her throat and nose when she made certain sounds.

Talking wasn't easy, but I did learn! My voice was never clear, but Annie and my family members could understand me. They **translated** my words so that I could communicate with other people.

Annie also taught me how to read **Braille**. I read every book I could. Annie even helped me study science and math.

Helen feels Annie Sullivan's lips move as she speaks.

Did you go to school?

Helen says: Annie and I had many of our lessons at my home. But we traveled too. Sometimes we visited a **boarding school** called the Perkins School for the Blind. And when I was fourteen, I began high school at the Wright-Humason School for the Deaf.

At school, I took English, math, and history classes. I listened to music too. Even though I couldn't hear, I could feel the vibrations of a piano or a violin.

After a few years, I moved to the Cambridge School for Young Ladies. Cambridge was a good school, but this school was for students who could hear and see.

Helen reads a book
written in Braille in 1899.

What was the Cambridge School like?

Helen says: It was wonderful! But it was also hard. I was the only blind and deaf person there. Luckily, Annie came to all my classes with me. She sat beside me and spelled the teacher's words into my hand. Later, I typed my notes on a Braille typewriter. It was also difficult to do my homework. I usually couldn't get Braille versions of the books I needed. Instead, Annie would read each book and spell the words in my hand.

Even though school was hard, I never gave up. With help from Annie and a private tutor, I finished high school. In 1900, when I was twenty years old, I made a big decision: I was going to college.

Helen *(left)* poses with Annie Sullivan. Annie made it possible for Helen to attend school.

Where did you go to college?

Helen says: I went to Radcliffe College. At the time, it was unusual for a woman to go to college at all. And it was very unusual for a woman with disabilities to go to college. I was the first deafblind college student in the country.

College was very hard, even though Annie came with me to all my classes. But in 1904, I became the first deafblind person to ever graduate from college. I was very proud.

Helen poses with her graduation cap and gown in 1904.

What did you do after college?

Helen says: I wrote many books. Some of my books were about my life. I wrote about what it was like to be blind and deaf.

I also wrote about my ideas. I believed all people are equal. But not everyone agreed with me. For example, the law said that women could not vote. I thought this was wrong. I wrote articles that said that women should vote just like men.

I worked for **civil rights** too. I believed African American people should be treated fairly. In 1916, I supported a new civil rights group called the National Association for the Advancement of Colored People, or the NAACP.

Helen works at her desk in 1911.

How did you become famous?

Helen says: Annie and I traveled around the world. I gave speeches about my life and my ideas in front of hundreds of people. Annie would translate my speeches for the audience. I became very popular. People all around the world came to hear me speak. In 1919, I even starred in a movie about my life!

Being famous wasn't always easy, though. A lot of people didn't like my ideas. Some people even said I didn't know what I was talking about. They said a deafblind person couldn't truly understand the world. But I worked hard to prove these people wrong. I always kept learning. This helped me explain and support my opinions.

Helen *(bottom right)* visits President John F. Kennedy *(bottom left)* on April 8, 1961.

What were your biggest successes?

Helen says: In 1915, I started Helen Keller International. This group works to prevent blindness around the world.

I also gave speeches to help raise money for the American Foundation for the Blind (AFB). People paid to attend my speeches, and the AFB used some of this money to record people reading books out loud. This way, blind people could listen to the books on **records**.

But I am most proud of the work I did with other blind people. During World War II, I visited soldiers in the hospital who had been blinded. I showed them that being blind wasn't a bad thing. I showed them how much blind people can do.

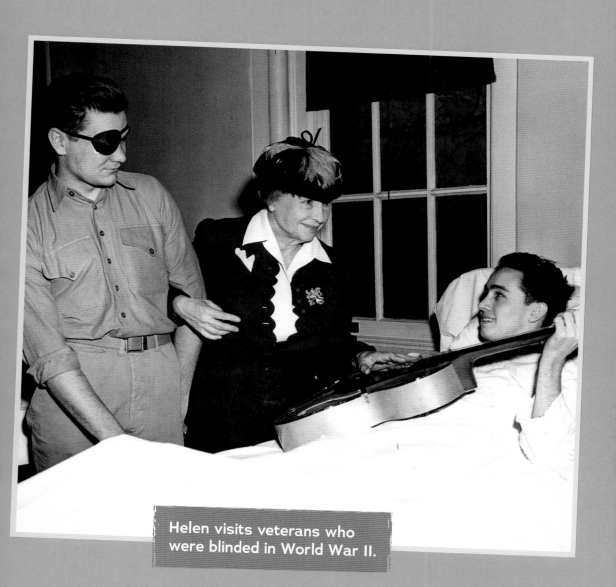

Helen visits veterans who were blinded in World War II.

How did your work help other people?

Helen says: When I was young, many deafblind people could not go to school or find jobs. But I showed the world that a deafblind person could live a full life. I went to college. I traveled the world. And I stood up for others who faced unfair treatment. I helped prove that people with disabilities can help themselves *and* help others, just like anyone else.

Timeline

1880:   Helen Keller is born in Alabama.

1882:   Helen becomes very sick, making her blind and deaf.

1887:   Annie Sullivan comes to the Keller farm to be Helen's teacher.

1903:   Helen publishes her first book, *The Story of My Life*. During her life, she wrote more than ten other books.

1904:   Helen graduates from Radcliffe College in Boston.

1913:   Helen gives her first public speech in Montclair, New Jersey.`

1915:   Helen starts Helen Keller International.`

1919:   Helen appears in a silent movie about her life called *Deliverance*.

1924:   Helen begins raising money for the American Foundation for the Blind.

1936:   Annie Sullivan dies of heart disease with Helen at her side.

1968:   Helen dies a few days after having a heart attack.

Glossary

activist: a person who fights for what he or she believes in

boarding school: a school where students live, eat, and sleep

Braille: a system of reading and writing for blind people. Letters are formed with small, raised dots.

civil rights: the rights of all people to be free and equal

disabilities: conditions that may damage or limit a person's physical or mental abilities

manual: something that is done with the hands

records: flat plastic discs that play music or other sounds

translated: changed from one language to another

vibrations: small, fast movements back and forth or from side to side

Further Information

Books

Boothroyd, Jennifer. *Vision: Nearsightedness, Farsightedness, and More*. Minneapolis: Lerner Publications, 2013. Read about sight and the genes that help decide how every person sees.

Kudlinski, Kathleen V. *Helen Keller: A Light for the Blind*. New York: Puffin, 2015. Learn more about Helen Keller; Annie Sullivan; and a friend of theirs, Polly Thomson.

Wilkie, Katharine. *Helen Keller*. New York: Aladdin, 2015. What was Helen like when she was a girl? This book explores Helen's childhood.

Websites

The American Foundation for the Blind: Braille Bug
http://braillebug.afb.org
Learn how to read Braille by playing fun games and sending secret messages.

The Perkins School: Helen Keller Facts
http://www.perkins.org/about/history/helen-keller-facts
This famous boarding school still teaches blind children. See pictures and read about Helen's life on their site.

Index

activist, 4
Alabama, 6
American Foundation for
    the Blind (AFB), 26

Braille, 14, 18

Cambridge School for
    Young Ladies, 16, 18
civil rights, 22

disabilities, 4, 10, 20, 28

manual alphabet, 12

National Association for
    the Advancement
    of Colored People
    (NAACP), 22

Perkins School for the
    Blind, 16

Radcliffe College, 20

Sullivan, Annie, 10, 12,
    14, 16, 18, 20, 24

Wright-Humason School
    for the Deaf, 16

Photo Acknowledgments

The images in this book are used with the permission of: © Bettmann/CORBIS, pp. 5, 9, 13, 21; Courtesy of Perkins School for the Blind, pp. 7 (top), 17, 27; © Ron S. Buskirk/Alamy, p. 7 (bottom); © BLM Collection/Alamy, p. 11; © Everett Collection/Alamy, p. 15; Library of Congress, p. 19; © Hulton-Deutsch/CORBIS, p. 23; © CORBIS, p. 25.

Front cover: Library of Congress.